100

words

every

4th grader

should

know

P9-CEL-638

THE 100 WORDS® *From the Editors of the*
AMERICAN HERITAGE®
DICTIONARIES

HOUGHTON MIFFLIN HARCOURT
Boston   New York

EDITORIAL AND PRODUCTION STAFF OF THE
American Heritage® Dictionaries

◆

BRUCE NICHOLS, *Senior Vice President, Publisher, General Interest Group*

STEVEN R. KLEINEDLER, *Executive Editor*

LOUISE E. ROBBINS, *Senior Editor*

PETER CHIPMAN, *Editor*

KATHERINE M. ISAACS, *Consulting Editor*

EMILY A. NEEVES, *Editorial Assistant*

CHRISTOPHER J. GRANNISS, *Database Production Supervisor*

MARGARET ANNE MILES, *Art and Production Supervisor*

SARAH IANI, *Associate Production Editor*

Visit our websites: hmhco.com *and* ahdictionary.com

LIBRARY OF CONGRESS CATALOGING-IN-PUBLICATION DATA
100 words every fourth grader should know /
From the Editors of the American Heritage Dictionaries.
pages cm. — (100 words)
ISBN 978-0-544-10611-6 (pbk.)
1. Vocabulary — Juvenile literature. I. Title: One hundred
words every fourth grader should know.
PE1449.A1423 2014
428.1 — dc23
2013023647

Text design by Anne Chalmers

MANUFACTURED IN THE UNITED STATES OF AMERICA

2 3 4 5 6 7 8 9 10 - DOC - 19 18 17 16 15

4500520288

Table of Contents

A Note to Teachers and Parents

Since 2002, the editors of the American Heritage® dictionaries have published over a dozen titles in the 100 Words® series, including *100 Words Every High School Graduate Should Know, 100 Words Almost Everyone Confuses and Misuses,* and *100 Words to Make You Sound Smart.* The response has been tremendous—over 800,000 copies have been sold, and we have received a great deal of positive feedback.

These books are intended to foster a love of language and to generate interest in dictionaries. Each title stands on its own, but in every book, we hope that the words selected will spur readers to explore the English language in greater depth. The full richness of the language is available at your fingertips in *The American Heritage® Dictionary of the English Language,* Fifth Edition, or online at ahdictionary.com. We are encouraged to see that so many people are aware of the importance of dictionaries for promoting literacy and vocabulary building.

Our readers have let us know that they're interested in a book in this series designed for younger children. We hope you will enjoy our newest title, *100 Words Every Fourth Grader Should Know,* a choice selection of words from A through Z that schoolchildren in the fourth grade (roughly ages 8 through 10) should be familiar with. We have chosen vocabulary words that are found in the reading materials that children of this age encounter at school and in the home.

Most of the definitions in this book are based on the *American Heritage® Children's Dictionary*. Example sentences show the use of these words in context. Quotations using these words come from popular authors of works for children, including Christopher Paul Curtis, E. L. Konigsburg, Ursula K. Le Guin, Grace Lin, Lois Lowry, Katherine Paterson, and E. B. White. In browsing through this book, your young student will build a larger vocabulary while getting a taste of many great works of children's literature.

We hope that you find sharing these words with your fourth grader to be a rewarding experience.

—**Steve Kleinedler**
Executive Editor

Guide to Parts of Speech

The parts of speech are the categories words fall into based on what role they play in the grammar of a sentence. The 100 words featured in this book belong to four parts of speech: *nouns, verbs, adjectives,* and *adverbs.*

NOUNS are words standing for people, places, objects, actions, or ideas. Examples of nouns include *acrobat, sofa, tidiness,* and *freedom.* Most nouns are usually singular but can be made plural (*acrobats, sofas,* and so on). If a noun is usually used in plural form, it is labeled as a **PLURAL NOUN.**

VERBS describe someone or something as doing something ("Sheep *eat* grass"), experiencing something ("My sister *suffers* from allergies"), or being in a particular state ("The pen *lay* on the table"). A grammatically complete sentence will usually contain at least one verb.

ADJECTIVES help to describe nouns by naming a quality of the person, place, or thing that the noun refers to. Examples of adjectives include *long* and *dark* in the phrase "a *long, dark* tunnel."

ADVERBS often describe the action in verbs by telling in what way something is done: "The waiter *sadly* informed us that the chowder was no longer available." They can also modify the meaning of an adjective: "an *incredibly* long, dark tunnel."

In addition to these four parts of speech, there are several other parts of speech that you ought to know about: *pronouns, prepositions, conjunctions, articles,* and *interjections.* None of these parts of speech appear among the 100 words featured in this book because most of the words belonging to these parts of speech are very basic words that are already familiar to you, even if you don't know what grammatical category they belong to.

PRONOUNS, such as *she, it,* and *themselves,* stand for nouns and play the same role nouns do in the grammar of a sentence.

PREPOSITIONS, such as *in, through,* and *with,* help to explain the relationship of a noun or verb to another noun. The relationship indicated by a preposition often but not always has to do with space ("the coats *in* the closet") or time ("slept *through* the night").

CONJUNCTIONS, such as *but* and *because,* help to join the parts of a sentence to each other.

ARTICLES, such as *an* and *the,* introduce nouns and tell whether the noun in question is general ("*a* heavy bookbag") or specific ("*the* heaviest bookbag in the world").

INTERJECTIONS, such as *yippee* and *hey,* don't play a role in the grammar of a sentence at all; they just express an emotion.

Guide to Pronunciation

This book shows how to say each word that is entered. A special spelling, called the *pronunciation*, appears in parentheses after the entry word. If a word has different pronunciations when it is used in different parts of speech, like *elaborate*, the pronunciation follows the part of speech label.

The letters and symbols in the pronunciation stand for the sounds in a word. You can see how to pronounce these letters and symbols by using the key that appears on the next page. The key has one special character (ə) that is called a *schwa*. The schwa is a vowel that is used in unstressed syllables, as in the first syllable of *ago* and the second syllable of *silent*.

Stress is greater loudness in a word or syllable compared with others that are spoken. Stress is shown in pronunciations by accent marks ′ (main stress) and ′ (lighter stress). Main stress is also shown by heavy, dark letters: **dictionary** (dĭk′shə nĕr′ē).

PRONUNCIATION KEY

Symbol	Examples	Symbol	Examples
ă	pat	oi	noise
ā	pay	ŏŏ	took
âr	care	ŏŏr	lure
ä	father	ōō	boot
b	bib	ou	out
ch	church	p	pop
d	deed, milled	r	roar
ĕ	pet	s	sauce
ē	bee	sh	ship, dish
f	fife, phase, rough	t	tight, stopped
		th	thin
g	gag	*th*	this
h	hat	ŭ	cut
hw	which	ûr	urge, term, firm, word, heard
ĭ	pit		
ī	pie, by		
îr	deer, pier	v	valve
j	judge	w	with
k	kick, cat, pique	y	yes
l	lid, needle	z	zebra, xylem
m	mum	zh	vision, pleasure, garage
n	no, sudden		
ng	thing		
ŏ	pot	ə	about, item, edible, gallop, circus
ō	toe		
ô	caught, paw		
ôr	core	ər	butter

When the Swan Boat docked and the passengers got off, long lines of people were waiting to get aboard for the next ride. Business was booming. Another boat was being made ready, to **accommodate** the crowds. Everyone wanted to ride the Swan Boats behind a real live swan playing a trumpet. It was the biggest happening in Boston in a long time.

—E. B. White, *The Trumpet of the Swan*

1

accommodate (ə kŏm′ə dāt′)

verb

1. To have room for someone or something; hold: *The auditorium can accommodate 500 people.* **2.** To do a favor or service for someone: *I wanted to pick up the cake the next day, but the baker could not accommodate me.*

2

afterthought (ăf′tər thôt′)

noun

An idea that occurs to a person after something else has been said or done: *They invited us to the birthday party, and as an afterthought, they said that we shouldn't bring a gift.*

> Sophie cast about for a weapon. The driver had gone off with his musket, but luckily some luggage had been fastened at the rear of the carriage. She seized a bunch of croquet mallets, a bag of billiard balls, and, as an **afterthought,** the Duchess' embroidery.
>
> —Joan Aiken, *Black Hearts in Battersea*

3

allegiance (ə lē′jəns)

noun

Loyalty to a country, a person, or a cause: *The knights pledged allegiance to the prince.*

> All is done in the King's name. But he would not be best pleased to find a real, live King of Narnia coming in upon him. And if your majesty came before him alone and un-armed—well he would not deny his **allegiance,** but he would pretend to disbelieve you.
> —C. S. Lewis, *The Voyage of the Dawn Treader*

4

aloft (ə lôft′)

adverb

High above the ground: *The first people to fly went aloft in balloons.*

> From either side the other two soldiers moved closer. The tall one stepped on the gun Jonathan had left. With a cry, he snatched it up and held it triumphantly **aloft.**
> —Avi, *The Fighting Ground*

5

ancestor (ăn′sĕs′tər)

noun

A person who was in your family long ago: *Some of my ancestors came to the United States from China.*

> A long time before this my **ancestors** had used the cave, why I do not know, and along the walls on each side they had cut figures in the stone. There were figures of pelicans floating in the water and flying, of dolphins, whales, sea elephants, gulls, ravens, dogs, and foxes. Near the opening of the cave they had also cut two deep basins in the stone, which I decided to use for storing water since they held much more than the baskets.
>
> —Scott O'Dell, *Island of the Blue Dolphins*

6

anticipation (ăn tĭs′ə pā′shən)

noun

1. The act of thinking of something in advance: *In anticipation of frost, we brought the plants inside.* **2.** The act of looking forward to something: *Everyone smiled with anticipation when the famous actor came out on the stage.*

> Rosa waved good-bye and headed for the bus stop. She fiddled in her pocket for the dime so that she would not have to ask for change. When she stepped up to drop her fare in, she was smiling in **anticipation** of the nice dinner she would make.
>
> —Nikki Giovanni, *Rosa*

7

antics (ăn′tĭks)

plural noun

Actions that get attention because they are funny or unusual: *The kittens' playful antics made us all laugh.*

Everywhere there were shops spilling wares out onto the street; bells and chants of hawkers; actors tumbling in front of small crowds, their costumed dogs barking at the **antics**; ladies holding their skirts above the churned mud.

—Gary D. Schmidt, *Anson's Way*

8

apparel (ə păr′əl)

noun

Clothing: *We bring summer apparel when we visit my grandparents in Florida.*

9

ascend (ə sĕnd′)

verb

To go up or move up: *The climbers ascended the mountain. The balloon ascended into the sky.*

> She led me up some wide stairs. As my eyes got used to the gloom I made out the shapes of the boarded windows, of dark doorways and broad landings. We **ascended** three stairways, passed three landings. Then the stairs narrowed and we came to a final narrow doorway.
>
> —David Almond, *Skellig*

> We sat beside each other by the fire, silent, watching the jewels change and glow first into white diamonds, then into sapphires, then into rubies. Sometimes Mrs. Baker got up and threw another piece of wood on the fire, and the sparks shattered up into the night darkness and we watched them **ascend** until they disappeared like the stuff of dreams.
>
> —Gary D. Schmidt, *The Wednesday Wars*

The slender Princess still wore at her throat the crescent moon of silver, and on her finger the ring crafted by the Fair Folk. But now a band of gold circled her brow, and the richness of her **apparel** made Taran suddenly aware of his travel-stained cloak and muddy boots.

—Lloyd Alexander, *The High King*

beckon (bĕk'ən)

verb

To signal with a movement of the head or hand:
The coach beckoned me to come over to the bench.

> The woman smiled and then **beckoned** Lissy to follow her
> to another room. Lissy followed the woman, and then we
> followed Lissy, like a parade.
>
> —Grace Lin, *Dumpling Days*

brink (brĭngk)

noun

1. The upper edge of a steep place: *From the brink of the cliff, you can look straight down.* **2.** The land bordering a body of water: *The ball stopped rolling just at the brink of the puddle.* **3.** The point when an event is about to occur: *He's on the brink of crying.*

> On they all went, leading their ponies, till they were brought to a good path and so at last to the very **brink** of the river. It was flowing fast and noisily, as mountain-streams do of a summer evening, when sun has been all day on the snow far up above.
>
> —J. R. R. Tolkien, *The Hobbit*

catastrophe (kə tăs′trə fē)

noun

An event, such as a flood, earthquake, or plane crash, that causes great suffering and damage: *Rescue crews responded quickly to the catastrophe.*

coax (kōks)

verb

1. To persuade someone by gentle urging or flattery: *Rachel coaxed me into lending her my bicycle by promising to return it in an hour.* **2.** To get something by coaxing: *I coaxed a smile from the baby.*

> I remember the night perfectly, maybe even a little bit clearer than it actually was, and don't doubt me when I tell you that as I stood gazing into the black woods behind the garage I felt a tugging, like someone right next to me was about to laugh, but there was no one. Small hands slid over mine, over the jar, **coaxing** me back to the woods.
>
> —Pam Conrad, *Stonewords: A Ghost Story*

Anne climbed the ladder amid breathless silence, gained the ridgepole, balanced herself uprightly on that precarious footing, and started to walk along it, dizzily conscious that she was uncomfortably high up in the world and that walking ridgepoles was not a thing in which your imagination helped you out much. Nevertheless, she managed to take several steps before the **catastrophe** came.

—L. M. Montgomery, *Anne of Green Gables*

compassion (kəm păsh′ən)

noun

A feeling of sharing someone else's suffering, together with a desire to help; deep sympathy: *Compassion led us to volunteer at the food pantry.*

> Jane Sharp became a midwife because she had given birth to six children (although none of them lived), went Sundays to Mass, and had strong hands and clean fingernails. She did her job with energy and some skill, but without care, **compassion,** or joy.
>
> —Karen Cushman, *The Midwife's Apprentice*

15

complexion (kəm plĕk′shən)

noun

The natural color of a person's skin, especially that of the face: *Which makeup is best for my complexion?*

> Darnell looked a lot like his sister, except that he was just a little lighter in **complexion**. He was the same coffee-brown tone as his mother, while Tamika was dark, like their father.
>
> —Walter Dean Myers, *Darnell Rock Reporting*

16

content (kən tĕnt′)

adjective

Happy with things the way they are; satisfied: *I wasn't content with the drawing I made, so I made another one.*

verb

To make someone content; satisfy: *The young boy contented himself by playing with his mother's phone.*

> It was not just an island. It was *the* island, waiting for them. It was their island. With an island like that within sight, who could be **content** to live on the mainland and sleep in a bed at night?
>
> —Arthur Ransome, *Swallows and Amazons*

17

courteous (kûr′tē əs)

adjective

Considerate toward other people; polite: *If you step on someone's toe, the courteous thing to do is apologize.*

> His face was quite calm and entirely **courteous**—but it was the distant, formal courtesy he always drew on like armor when he had to deal with people he disliked.
>
> —Elizabeth Marie Pope, *The Sherwood Ring*

18

cringe (krĭnj)

verb

To shiver or move your body suddenly out of fear, pain, embarrassment, or disgust: *Kayla cringed when the dog growled at her.*

> Maniac uncrumpled the page, flattened it out as best he could. How could he return the book to Amanda in this condition? He couldn't. But he had to. It was hers. Judging from that morning, she was pretty finicky about her books. What would make her madder—to not get the book back at all, or to get it back with a page ripped out? Maniac **cringed** at both prospects.
>
> —Jerry Spinelli, *Maniac Magee*

derelict (dĕr′ə lĭkt′)

adjective

1. Deserted by an owner; abandoned: *The derelict garage was finally torn down.* **2.** Neglectful: *A good police officer is never derelict in his or her duty.*

> She started crying. She said we should never have left Random Road. We should never have come to this stinking **derelict** place.
> —David Almond, *Skellig*

dignity (dĭg′nĭ tē)

noun

The fact of being or appearing worthy of respect or honor: *Your brother may have failed the test, but at least he kept his dignity by not cheating.*

"What are you doing trespassing in my cabin?"
I asked the question with as much **dignity** as I
could muster while spitting out leaves, brush-
ing off my clothes, and getting to my feet.

—Katherine Paterson, *Preacher's Boy*

21

distaste (dĭs tāst′)

noun

A feeling of not liking something: *I looked with distaste at the plate of undercooked eggs.*

> When he returned to the classroom, he saw a large box with several smaller ones in front of the room. Mrs. Hamlin was crouched over the large one. With an expression of **distaste** on her face, she examined its contents.
>
> —Candy Dawson Boyd, *Chevrolet Saturdays*

22

dormant (dôr′mənt)

adjective

Not active for a time: *The volcano is dormant at the moment, but it could still erupt in the future.*

> Except for the green of pines that mottled the mountainside, the forests stood barren. There must have been a fire, Boy thought. Still, their trunks were not blackened; they just looked **dormant,** like trees in winter.
>
> —Belinda Hurmence, *A Girl Called Boy*

23

elaborate

adjective (ĭ lăb'ər ĭt)

Having many complicated parts or details: *The crew constructed elaborate sets for the play.*

verb (ĭ lăb'ə rāt')

To say more about something; give details: *The speaker first gave a general idea of her subject and then elaborated on each of the important points.*

> The whole household seemed so reasonable, she had to keep reminding herself it was all a stage setting in some kind of **elaborate** dream.
>
> —Jane Yolen, *The Devil's Arithmetic*

endure (ĕn dŏŏr′)

verb

1. To continue to exist; last: *Their friendship endured for years.* **2.** To put up with something; tolerate: *I can no longer endure your rudeness.*

> He felt he could scarcely **endure** another meal of plain fish. He was hungry for a bit of something tasty.
>> —Elizabeth George Speare, *The Sign of the Beaver*

enforce (ĕn fôrs′)

verb

To make sure that something is obeyed: *The principal has to enforce the school's rules.*

> Officer Ken smiled. "We tend to look the other way when it's in a residential neighborhood. But right here, on the town green, we have to **enforce** the law."
>> —Jacqueline Davies, *The Lemonade War*

exertion (ĭg zûr′shən)

noun

The act of working hard at something: *The wheelbarrow allowed us to move the rocks with very little exertion.*

> Gregor began to pant, but the roaches didn't show any visible signs of **exertion**. He had no idea how far they were going. Their destination could be a hundred miles away. Who knew how far these things could run?
>
> —Suzanne Collins, *Gregor the Overlander*

expanse (ĭk spăns′)

noun

A wide and open area: *The Sahara is a vast expanse of desert.*

> He had never hunted tigers in India, or climbed the peaks of the Himalayas, or dived for pearls in the South Seas. Above all, he had never seen the Poles. That was what he regretted most of all. He had never seen those great shining white **expanses** of ice and snow.
>
> —Richard and Florence Atwater, *Mr. Popper's Penguins*

extraordinary (ĭk strôr′dn ĕr′ē *or* ĕk′strə ôr′dn ĕr′ē)

adjective

Very unusual; remarkable: *Landing on the moon was an extraordinary accomplishment.*

> Everybody in Billings bought a copy of the paper and read all about the **extraordinary** event. It was talked about all over town. Some people believed it; others said it never could have happened. They said the store owner had just invented it to get some publicity for his store. But the clerks in the store agreed that it had really happened. They pointed to the drops of blood on the floor.
>
> —E. B. White, *The Trumpet of the Swan*

foliage (fō′lē ĭj)

noun

The leaves of trees or other plants: *Gardeners grow some plants for their flowers and others for their foliage.*

Knowing I couldn't turn my dogs loose, I broke off enough of the wire to lead them. As I passed under the branches of the bur oak tree, I looked up into the dark **foliage.** I could see the bright eyes of the ghost coon. Everything that had happened on this terrible night was because of his very existence, but it wasn't his fault.

—Wilson Rawls, *Where the Red Fern Grows*

Yuki liked Mr. Toda better than the seminary students because he was more open about his feelings. If he liked you, he let you know, and if he didn't, he was equally **frank**. Yuki liked people like that. She knew that the old man liked her too.

—Yoshiko Uchida, *Journey to Topaz*

foremost (fôr′mōst′)

adjective

First in rank, position, or importance; chief: *Shakespeare is the foremost playwright in English literature.*

> Lynn planned to become either a rocket scientist or a famous writer. Though I knew nothing about animals, she said that when I grew up I would go to Africa to study them. I can't say that the idea of college was **foremost** on my mind; nevertheless, if Lynn was going, I would too.
>
> —Cynthia Kadohata, *Kira-Kira*

frank (frăngk)

adjective

Free and open in expressing thoughts and feelings; honest: *Give me your frank opinion of my haircut.*

function (fŭngk′shən)

noun

1. The proper activity of a person or thing; a purpose or use: *The function of a thermometer is to measure temperature.* **2.** A formal social gathering or official ceremony, like a wedding.

verb

To have or perform a function; serve: *This post functions as a support. My printer isn't functioning right.*

> Without warning, coming as a complete and unexpected shock, she felt a pressure she had never imagined, as though she were being completely flattened out by an enormous steamroller.... She tried to gasp, but a paper doll can't gasp. She thought she was trying to think, but her flattened-out mind was as unable to **function** as her lungs.
>
> —Madeleine L'Engle, *A Wrinkle in Time*

33

futile (fyo͞ot'l *or* fyo͞o'tīl)

adjective

Having no useful results; useless: *I made a futile effort to recover the file that I had accidentally erased on my computer.*

> I suggest you not attempt to escape the energy cage. You will find the experience both **futile** and rather painful.
>
> —Deva Fagan, *Circus Galacticus*

34

gaze (gāz)

verb

To look at something steadily and for a long time: *They gazed in wonder at the high mountains.*

noun

A long, steady look: *The judge fixed her gaze on the defendant.*

> Mari walks up the slight incline behind the trailer to the field where the cows graze. The moon is on the wane, but it's still a pie with half its pieces left, so there is enough light to watch her by. Midfield, she stops and **gazes** up at the sky, slowly turning west, south, east, full circle.
>
> —Julia Alvarez, *Return to Sender*

glimmer (glĭm′ər)

noun

1. A dim, unsteady light: *I could barely see the red glimmer of the coals.* **2.** A faint indication; a trace: *We had a glimmer of hope.*

verb

To shine with a dim, unsteady light: *A candle glimmered in the distant window.*

> They went on, down and down with the running water, Curdie getting more and more afraid it was leading them to some terrible gulf in the heart of the mountain. In one or two places he had to break away the rock to make room before even Irene could get through—at least without hurting herself. But at length they spied a **glimmer** of light, and in a minute more, they were almost blinded by the full sunlight into which they emerged.
>
> —George MacDonald, *The Princess and the Goblin*

glimpse (glĭmps)

noun

A very quick look: *We caught a glimpse of the house as we drove by.*

verb

To get a quick look at something: *Hannah glimpsed one of her friends in the crowd.*

> Joel reached the bottom of the hill and shot across the bridge so fast that he didn't get even a **glimpse** of the river below.
>
> —Marion Dane Bauer, *On My Honor*

grimace (grĭm′ĭs)

noun

A twisting or contortion of the face, usually from disgust or pain: *He made a grimace when he smelled the rotting food.*

verb

To twist or contort the face, usually from disgust or pain: *She grimaced with pain as she pulled out the splinter.*

> Reuven stood on the platform waving, waving like crazy. He could not make himself smile. He tried, but each time his lips pressed together into a **grimace**.
>
> —Kathryn Lasky, *Broken Song*

38

headstrong (hĕd′strông′)

adjective

Determined to have your own way; stubborn: *Jacob is so headstrong that it's useless to argue with him.*

> Lots of other mill girls were jealous of her beauty and said spiteful things to and about her, but she only tossed her head and laughed in their faces. She was as **headstrong** and smart as she was handsome.
>
> —Patricia Beatty, *Turn Homeward, Hannalee*

39

hesitate (hĕz′ĭ tāt′)

verb

To be slow to act, speak, or decide because of feeling unsure; pause: *I hesitated before diving off the high board. Please don't hesitate to ask a question if there's something you don't understand.*

> She thanked the small gentleman for his trouble. He bowed, **hesitated** as if he meant to say something further, then seemed to think better of it, and drove away.
>
> —Edward Eager, *Half Magic*

In the silence, **immense,** dark, overwhelming, shouldering over the road, towering like castles, the great trees rose and pressed about the horses and their riders, melting away on every side into depth on depth of green shadow that opened a little to let them through and then closed in behind them again.

—Elizabeth Marie Pope, *The Perilous Gard*

40

hoist (hoist)

verb

To lift or haul something up, especially by pulling from above: *The crane hoisted the beam into position.*

> The old man gathered his own bones and muscles as best he could and managed to **hoist** the kid and get him into the pickup. He laid him on the seat, bent his legs so he could close the door.
>
> —Jerry Spinelli, *Maniac Magee*

41

immense (ĭ měns′)

adjective

Of great size, extent, or degree: *Antarctica is covered by an immense sheet of ice.*

42

imperceptibly (ĭm′pər sĕp′tə blē)

adverb

In a way that is impossible to notice: *From one day to the next, the pond looked the same, but we could tell over time that it was drying up imperceptibly.*

> He leaned back a little and pushed—almost **imperceptibly**—against the door with his shoulders: it opened sweetly, in its silent way. Not one of the men had looked up.
>
> —Mary Norton, *The Borrowers*

43

indication (ĭn′dĭ kā′shən)

noun

Something that indicates; a sign: *A wrinkled forehead may be an indication of worry or deep thought.*

> They found a wide gateway open and passed through it into a paved courtyard. And it was here that they had their first **indication** that there was something odd about this island. In the middle of the courtyard stood a pump, and beneath the pump a bucket. There was nothing odd about that. But the pump handle was moving up and down, though there seemed to be no one moving it.
>
> —C. S. Lewis, *The Voyage of the Dawn Treader*

44

inscription (ĭn skrĭp′shən)

noun

1. The act of writing or carving on a surface: *The inscription of the message must have been done with a chisel.* **2.** Something that is written or carved on a surface: *An interesting inscription is on the gate.*

> That's when I realized where I was. The mossy rocks I'd noticed before were tombstones. Most were so old they blended into the trees and bushes, their **inscriptions** worn and covered with lichen.
>
> —Mary Downing Hahn, *Deep and Dark and Dangerous*

45

instinctive (ĭn stĭngk′tĭv)

adjective

Being an inherited behavior rather than a learned one: *Humans have an instinctive ability to learn languages.*

> When an animal gets backed into a corner, zoologists say the animal will usually choose one of three **instinctive** responses. But I've never considered myself an animal.
>
> —Andrew Clements, *The Report Card*

intent (ĭn tĕnt′)

noun

A purpose or aim; an intention: *Was it your intent to start an argument?*

adjective

1. Having the mind or thoughts set on a goal; determined: *He is intent on finishing the marathon.* **2.** Showing close attention: *The judge listened with an intent expression on her face.*

> I would have liked to follow him myself, but I would quickly have been missed and so had to remain in camp. How was I to find out Seth's **intent** and the reason he was keeping company with a wasp?
>
> —Mark Copeland, *The Bundle at Blackthorpe Heath*

interior (ĭn tîr′ē ər)

noun

An inner part; the inside: *The interior of the earth is extremely hot.*

adjective

Having to do with or located on the inside; inner: *This paint is for the interior walls of your house.*

He tiptoed timidly up the three wooden steps to the door, tapped lightly, and leaped back in fright, for the moment he knocked there was a terrible crash inside the wagon that sounded as if a whole set of dishes had been dropped from the ceiling onto a hard stone floor. At the same time the door flew open, and from the dark **interior** a hoarse voice inquired, "Have you ever heard a whole set of dishes dropped from the ceiling onto a hard stone floor?"

—Norton Juster, *The Phantom Tollbooth*

Thomas ran smack into a wall. His arms and hands hit first; then, his head and chest. The impact **jarred** him from head to foot.

—Virginia Hamilton, *The House of Dies Drear*

48

jar (jär)

verb

1. To bump or shake something strongly: *The explosion jarred buildings for miles around.* **2.** To startle or upset someone: *We were jarred by the news that the famous baseball player had died.*

49

keepsake (kēp′sāk′)

noun

Something that is kept in memory of a person or an occasion: *Jessica saved her grandmother's favorite coffee mug as a keepsake.*

> Children were not allowed to bring any **keepsakes** with them, although some managed to smuggle a beloved photograph or locket on the journey west.
>
> —Andrea Warren, *Orphan Train Rider*

knack (năk)

noun

A special talent or skill: *My mom has a knack for fixing things around the house.*

> Poor Fern. She didn't have the **knack** for counting. . . . She couldn't get past twenty copies without losing her place and had to start over, again and again.
> —Rita Williams-Garcia, *One Crazy Summer*

literacy (lĭt′ər ə sē)

noun

1. The ability to read and write: *The library has just started a story hour to help promote literacy.*
2. Good understanding of a certain field: *This job requires computer literacy.*

> A learner soon became a teacher, and new learners became new teachers. **Literacy** spread in this natural way, without desks or drills or schoolrooms.
> —Janet Klausner, *Sequoyah's Gift: A Portrait of the Cherokee Leader*

lurch (lûrch)

verb

To move suddenly and unsteadily: *We all lurched forward when the car swerved.*

> Yuki waved and waved as the bus **lurched** down the dusty road. She kept waving even when she knew her friends could no longer see her and they became small black dots in the sand. She watched the black barracks and the hospital and the watchtowers grow smaller and smaller, until soon they were only a splotch in the desert.
>
> —Yoshiko Uchida, *Journey to Topaz*

makeshift (māk′shĭft′)

adjective

Serving as a temporary substitute for something else: *We used the lid of the trash can as a makeshift sled.*

> Each morning when they came out of their tent, they could see that other families had come to join the **makeshift** camp. There were no more proper tents, so the new arrivals had to make do with plastic sheets hung over chestnut tree branches and propped up with sticks.
>
> —Katherine Paterson, *The Day of the Pelican*

malicious (mə lĭsh′əs)

adjective

Feeling or showing a desire to hurt others; spiteful: *Someone started a malicious rumor about the teacher.*

> She did not smile, but something lightened in her eyes—a **malicious** gleam, a look of triumph. She carried a candle which shone upwards on her face, streaking it strangely with light and shadow. "What are you doing down here?" she asked.
>
> —Mary Norton, *The Borrowers*

massive (măs′ĭv)

adjective

Large, heavy, and solid; bulky: *A massive boulder blocked the road.*

meager (mē′gər)

adjective

Small in quantity; barely enough: *Kendra complained about her meager allowance.*

> The most relentless of his new fears was that they would starve. Now that they had left the cultivated fields behind them, it was almost impossible to find food. They finished the **meager** store of potatoes and carrots they had saved from the last agricultural area, and now they were always hungry.
>
> —Lois Lowry, *The Giver*

The ride was noisy, bumpy, and thrilling. When they stopped for a light before going onto the freeway, Joey was amazed that the truck filled the entire lane. At the same time, he fretted about how the **massive** machine would handle the speed of the freeway.

—Candy Dawson Boyd, *Chevrolet Saturdays*

melancholy (mĕl′ən kŏl′ē)

adjective

Sad; gloomy: *The violinist played a melancholy song.*

noun

Low spirits; sadness: *The sale of my grandparents' farm filled me with melancholy.*

Now there was nothing left but to get ready to leave Arundel. They had to organize and pack and clean, all those **melancholy** end-of-vacation chores that take so much longer than they should.

—Jeanne Birdsall, *The Penderwicks*

58

merge (mûrj)

verb

1. To bring two or more things together in order to form a single unit; unite: *The owners decided to merge the two companies.* **2.** To come together: *The rivers run parallel before they merge.*

> The cleared land gave again to forest and his voice echoed through the woodland, **merging** with the singing of birds, the running of a brook, the clopping of a horse's hooves.
>
> —Elizabeth Yates, *Amos Fortune, Free Man*

59

mingle (mĭng′gəl)

verb

1. To mix or become mixed; combine: *The smell of coffee mingled with the smell of fried eggs in the kitchen.* **2.** To join in company with others: *We mingled with the crowd during the play's intermission.*

> As he entered the water clouds crossed the sun's face and great shadows slid and **mingled** over the water of the pool about him. He crossed to the far bank, shuddering with cold but walking slow and erect as he should through that icy, living water.
>
> —Ursula K. Le Guin, *A Wizard of Earthsea*

minuscule (mĭn′ə skyo͞ol′)

adjective

Very small; tiny: *Our plan had only a minuscule chance of success.*

> The pages of the diary began to blow as though caught in a high wind, stopping halfway through the month of June. Mouth hanging open, Harry saw that the little square for June thirteenth seemed to have turned into a **minuscule** television screen.
>
> —J. K. Rowling, *Harry Potter and the Chamber of Secrets*

momentary (mō′mən tĕr′ē)

adjective

Lasting only for a short period of time: *The sun shown briefly during a momentary break in the clouds.*

> Like some animal that doesn't know how to climb a tree, never has known how to climb a tree, but thinks it will just try anyway, the bear went up the trunk by main force; and he didn't so much climb down as fall, interrupting his plunge with five or six desperate **momentary** pauses.
>
> —Randall Jarrell, *The Animal Family*

nape (nāp)

noun

The back of the neck: *Mother cats carry their kittens by the nape of the neck.*

> I watch the reverend from behind. His thick shoulders force the seams of his black suit. As soon as the reverend turns to Luke 2:1–20, his whole stance changes. All of him goes tense. His hand clamps the back of his neck. Here we are in this chilly church, and the reverend wipes his **nape** with his hankie.
>
> —Andrea Davis Pinkney, *Bird in a Box*

nimble (nĭm′bəl)

adjective

1. Moving quickly, lightly, and easily: *The nimble cat jumped up on the fence.* **2.** Quick and clever in thinking, learning, or answering: *It takes a nimble mind to do well on a quiz show.*

obstinate (ŏb′stə nĭt)

adjective

Feeling or displaying an unwillingness to give in: *I wanted to go to the movies, but my brother was obstinate about staying home.*

> Bonnie left her perch reluctantly enough and came to sit by the fire. She was a slender creature, small for her age, but rosy-cheeked, with a mass of tumbled black locks falling to her shoulders, and two brilliant blue eyes, equally ready to dance with laughter or flash with indignation. Her square chin also gave promise of a powerful and **obstinate** temper, not always perfectly controlled.
>
> —Joan Aiken, *The Wolves of Willoughby Chase*

Magic shut the gates, but he could sometimes get out, if he was quick. Companies of the Wood-elves, sometimes with the king at their head, would from time to time ride out to hunt, or to other business in the woods and in the lands to the East. Then if Bilbo was very **nimble,** he could slip out just behind them; though it was a dangerous thing to do.

—J. R. R. Tolkien, *The Hobbit*

65

opt (ŏpt)

verb

To make a choice or decision about something:
We opted to walk instead of driving.

> Mom immediately ordered a bratwurst with sauerkraut and
> peppers, even though we had just eaten lunch at home. My
> father **opted** for the homemade vanilla ice cream smoth-
> ered with fresh strawberries. And Emily and I found our-
> selves in front of the cotton candy booth.
>
> —Lisa Yee, *Millicent Min, Girl Genius*

66

overwhelming (ō′vər wĕl′mĭng)

adjective

1. Easily defeating or overpowering an enemy
or opponent: *Our team's overwhelming offense
brought us victory.* **2.** Affecting someone very
strongly; too much for someone: *The humidity
was overwhelming—I just had to lie down.*

> Neftalí reached out and hugged Mamadre's neck tight. He
> wanted to tell her how much he loved her. He wanted to tell
> her he was sorry for being angry with her and not talking
> to her. But his **overwhelming** emotions stood in the way of
> his words.
>
> —Pam Muñoz Ryan, *The Dreamer*

67

pact (păkt)

noun

A formal agreement, especially between nations; a treaty: *The leaders signed a pact to ban testing of nuclear weapons.*

> Outside in the corridor, we made a **pact** that we wouldn't tell any of the other children about what we had seen. Mr. Snoddy had always been kind to us, and we wanted to repay him by keeping his deep dark secret to ourselves.
>
> —Roald Dahl, *Danny the Champion of the World*

68

pandemonium (păn′də **mō**′nē əm)

noun

A condition or scene of noisy confusion: *There was pandemonium when the doors to the concert opened and the crowd rushed in.*

> Below was **pandemonium**. It seemed as though half of Helsinki's inhabitants had already managed to launch themselves in various crafts, and a veritable flotilla was heading toward the explosion site, led by a coast guard vessel, two powerful outboards churning at its stern, nose up for speed.
>
> —Eoin Colfer, *Artemis Fowl: The Time Paradox.*

persuade (pər swād′)

verb

To talk someone into doing or believing something; convince: *We finally persuaded them that they were wrong.*

phenomenal (fĭ nŏm′ə nəl)

adjective

Remarkable; extraordinary: *A cheetah can run at a phenomenal speed.*

I give a little test bounce. The entire Ring is a kind of giant trampoline. No wonder the Clowns could manage those **phenomenal** leaps.

—Deva Fagan, *Circus Galacticus*

More even than she hated cooked things, the mermaid hated anything sweet. Once the hunter **persuaded** her to try some berries: she sniffed uncertainly at them, put them in her mouth, and then spat them out, exclaiming: "They're ugly, ugly! All gummy and blurry! How can you eat them?"

—Randall Jarrell, *The Animal Family*

ponder (pŏn′dər)

verb

To think about something carefully; consider:
*Alyssa pondered the meaning of her dream. Noah
pondered over the decision.*

> Mary looked at the fire and **pondered** a little. She must
> be careful if she meant to keep her secret kingdom. She
> wasn't doing any harm, but if Mr. Craven found out about
> the open door he would be fearfully angry and get a new
> key and lock it up forevermore. She really could not bear
> that.
>
> —Frances Hodgson Burnett, *The Secret
> Garden*

quantity (kwŏn′tĭ tē)

noun

An amount or number of a thing or things:
*Trains transport large quantities of farm goods
each year.*

> Food, all food, even food he did not like, never lost its won-
> der for him. For years after his rescue he would find him-
> self stopping in grocery stores to just stare at the aisles of
> food, marveling at the **quantity** and the variety.
>
> —Gary Paulsen, *Hatchet*

quaver (kwā'vər)

verb

To be unsteady in pitch or volume: *His voice quavered as he spoke in front of the large crowd.*

> The Archmage Nemmerle, Warder of Roke, was an old man, older it was said than any man then living. His voice **quavered** like the bird's voice when he spoke, welcoming Ged kindly.

> —Ursula K. Le Guin, *A Wizard of Earthsea*

quench (kwĕnch)

verb

1. To satisfy a thirst by drinking something: *I quenched my thirst with a glass of cold water.* **2.** To put out a fire; extinguish: *We quenched the campfire with a bucket of water.*

> That night they ate their very last scraps and crumbs of food; and next morning when they woke the first thing they noticed was that they were still gnawingly hungry, and the next thing was that it was raining and that here and there the drip of it was dropping heavily on the forest floor. That only reminded them that they were also parchingly thirsty, without doing anything to relieve them: you cannot **quench** a terrible thirst by standing under giant oaks and waiting for a chance drip to fall on your tongue.
>
> —J. R. R. Tolkien, *The Hobbit*

radiant (rā′dē ənt)

adjective

1. Giving off light or heat: *The radiant glow from the fireplace made the room cozy.* **2.** Showing or indicating love or happiness: *The children had radiant smiles.*

ravine (rə vēn′)

noun

A small valley with steep sides made by running water: *The hikers descended into the ravine, where it was cool and dark.*

> This place lay on a headland a half league to the west of Coral Cove. There was a large rock on that headland and two stunted trees. Behind the rock was a clear place about ten steps across, which was sheltered from the wind, from which I could see the harbor and the ocean. A spring of water flowed from a **ravine** nearby.
>
> —Scott O'Dell, *Island of the Blue Dolphins*

As Ms. Ramírez spoke, Tyler's gaze was drawn to Mari's face, which seemed suddenly lit up from inside like a jack-o'-lantern. Some memory was making her look **radiant**.

—Julia Alvarez, *Return to Sender*

recipient (rĭ sĭp′ē ənt)

noun

Someone who receives something: *She has been the recipient of many awards for her music.*

> I did not speak to him for the rest of the day, and when he left the pool to return to the condo for lunch, I did not go with him. I thought that it would do him good to know how it felt to be the **recipient** rather than the giver of silence.
>
> —E. L. Konigsburg, *The View from Saturday*

resentful (rĭ zĕnt′fŭl)

adjective

Angry or bitter about something someone has done to you: *Daniel was resentful about not being chosen to sing in the musical.*

> Her voice had the same sugary sweet tone she had started with, but the words were bitter and **resentful**. All of a sudden it was like I was trying to steal something from her—something I wasn't good enough to have.
>
> —Aaron Hawkins, *The Year Money Grew on Trees*

satisfactory (săt′ĭs făk′tə rē)

adjective

Good enough but not the best; adequate: *Your work was satisfactory, but I know that you can do better.*

The Directors thought hard, did much scratching of their heads and made many ridiculous suggestions, but were unable to think of any **satisfactory** ideas on such short notice.

—William Pene du Bois, *The Twenty-One Balloons*

sensitive (sĕn′sĭ tĭv)

adjective

1. Aware of or having sympathy for the feelings of others: *Because my teacher is sensitive to others' feelings, she doesn't allow any teasing in the classroom.* **2.** Quick to have your feelings hurt; touchy: *Brandon is too sensitive to criticism.* **3.** Easily irritated: *Babies have sensitive skin.* **4.** Able to perceive something through the senses: *Dogs' ears are sensitive to sounds that most humans can't hear.*

> A short, round boy of seven, he took little interest in troublesome things, preferring to remain on good terms with everyone. Yet he was always **sensitive** to others and now, shifting the handle of his lunch can from his right hand to his right wrist and his smudged notebook from his left hand to his left armpit, he stuffed his free hands into his pockets and attempted to make his face as moody as Stacey's and as cranky as mine.
>
> —Mildred D. Taylor, *Roll of Thunder, Hear My Cry*

Mary had never possessed an animal pet of her own and had always thought she should like one. So she began to feel a slight interest in Dickon, and as she had never before been interested in any one but herself, it was the dawning of a healthy **sentiment**.

—Frances Hodgson Burnett,
The Secret Garden

sentiment (sĕn′tə mənt)

noun

1. A tender, romantic, or passionate feeling about something: *The march music stirred up their patriotic sentiment.* **2.** A general opinion or view: *The sentiment of the community is that we need more public parks.*

shudder (shŭd′ər)

verb

To tremble or shiver suddenly, especially from fear or cold: *We all shuddered as we went into the dark cave.*

> The judge came in and sat down and we did the same. Skyla and Clive on one side and Gram, Owen, and I on the other. Even though the judge looked friendly with smile wrinkles around her eyes like Fabiola's, as soon as I saw that black robe, I **shuddered** inside. It meant the law, that whatever the judge said would have to be carried out.
>
> —Pam Muñoz Ryan, *Becoming Naomi León*

sickly (sĭkʹlē)

adjective

1. Tending to become sick; frail: *One puppy was sickly and kept apart from the others.* **2.** Resembling or seeming like a symptom of sickness: *The sky turned a sickly green before the tornado struck.*

> In general, I avoided looking at myself much in the mirror, but when I did get a glimpse during those days, I could see my eyes had deep black circles around them. The rest of my face had a **sickly** color with my nose and the whites of my eyes looking a bloodshot red.
>
> —Aaron Hawkins, *The Year Money Grew on Trees*

sleek (slēk)

adjective

Very smooth and glossy: *The horse has a sleek coat.*

> All day the sun beat hot on the house. All day it was full of the crawling sound that went up the wall and over the roof and down. All day grasshoppers' heads with bulging eyes, and grasshoppers' legs clutching, were thick along the bottom edge of the shut windows; all day they tried to walk up the **sleek** glass and fell back, while thousands more pushed up and tried and fell.
>
> —Laura Ingalls Wilder, *On the Banks of Plum Creek*

solemn (sŏl′əm)

adjective

1. Very serious; grave: *A funeral is a solemn occasion.* **2.** Made or taken after serious thought and with an understanding of possible consequences: *Sophia made a solemn promise never to reveal the secret.*

> They were to be allowed to use the sailing boat by themselves. They were to be allowed to sail out from the little sheltered bay, and round the point, and down the lake to the island. They were to be allowed to land on the island, and to live there until it was time to pack up again and go home to town and school and lessons. The news was so good that it made them **solemn**. They ate their bread and marmalade in silence.
>
> —Arthur Ransome, *Swallows and Amazons*

soothe (so͞o*th*)

verb

1. To make someone or something calm or quiet: *The sound of the music soothed the restless baby.* **2.** To make something less painful; relieve: *Warm tea will soothe your sore throat.*

stagger (stăg′ər)

verb

1. To walk unsteadily: *The bear woke up and staggered out of its den.* **2.** To overwhelm someone, as with amazement: *The size of the building staggered us.* **3.** To arrange something in alternating rows or time periods: *The seats were staggered so that everyone could see the stage.*

> When his team was out in the field, the boys made Lewis play right field, because not many balls got hit out that way. But when one did, Lewis always dropped it, unless it hit him on the head. He would **stagger** back and forth as he tried to keep track of the ball that hung there, high over his head, but he always got dizzy and covered his face with his glove and screamed "No! No!" as the ball came down.
>
> —John Bellairs, *The House with a Clock in its Walls*

And off the midwife ran, up to the manor where warm fires blazed and the laboring mother was **soothed** with wine and syrups and kind words. Alyce turned back to the dark, cold, nearly empty cottage, took a deep breath, and went in.

—Karen Cushman, *The Midwife's Apprentice*

88

stern (stûrn)

adjective

Serious or strict: *The lifeguard gave us a stern warning against swimming too far from the shore.*

You might think, if you didn't know him well, that he was a **stern** and serious man. He wasn't. He was actually a wildly funny person. What made him appear so serious was the fact that he never smiled with his mouth. He did it all with his eyes. He had brilliant blue eyes and when he thought of something funny, his eyes would flash and, if you looked carefully, you could actually see a tiny little golden spark dancing in the middle of each eye. But the mouth never moved.

—Roald Dahl, *Danny the Champion of the World*

tantalize (tăn′tə līz′)

verb

To excite someone by presenting something desirable while keeping it out of reach: *Scientists have been tantalized by the possibility of finding a cure for cancer.*

> A woman came out of one of the nearby cottages, carrying a basket of small loaves of bread, and with them the new-baked smell that had so **tantalized** Will before.
>
> —Susan Cooper, *The Dark Is Rising*

temptation (tĕmp tā′shən)

noun

1. The act of tempting or the state of being tempted: *We gave in to temptation and ate all the cookies.* **2.** Something that tempts: *A cool swim on a hot day was too great a temptation to resist.*

> "Kenny, we've done all we can and it seems the **temptations** are just too much for By here in Flint. So hopefully, the slower pace in Alabama will help him by removing some of those temptations."
>
> —Christopher Paul Curtis, *The Watsons Go to Birmingham—1963*

transform (trăns fôrm′)

verb

1. To change the form or appearance of someone or something by a large amount: *The snow completely transformed the landscape.* **2.** To change the nature, function, or condition of something; convert: *A steam engine transforms heat into power.*

An hour later, Jessie and Megan had **transformed** the little wooden puppet theater in Megan's basement into the hottest new lemonade stand on the block.

—Jacqueline Davies, *The Lemonade War*

unscrupulous (ŭn skrōo′pyə ləs)

adjective

Not honest or trustworthy: *We watched a movie about an unscrupulous businessman who cheated his partners.*

In ancient, more honest times, a man could only earn the title of scholar after years of long study and passing three exams, each one harder than the last one. However, owning even the lowest scholarly title—whether earned or bought—gave the holder and his clan certain advantages. For one thing, **unscrupulous** people like the Phoenixes could use the title to get out of certain kinds of taxes; but more importantly, it made it easier for the Phoenixes to see the government officials who were "brother" scholars.

—Laurence Yep, *The Serpent's Children*

vain (vān)

adjective

1. Too proud of your appearance or accomplishments; conceited: *He was a vain person who always talked about himself.* **2.** Unsuccessful; futile: *Firefighters made a vain attempt to save the burning building.*

vengeance (vĕn′jəns)

noun

The act of trying to hurt someone who has hurt you; revenge: *The king vowed to take vengeance on the prince who had tried to overthrow him.*

> He thought of his sister Shriprinka, his mother and father, and he thought of the music, the song begun long ago in the shtetl, broken by blood and **vengeance** in the horror of a single night.
>
> —Kathryn Lasky, *Broken Song*

I don't have anything to be **vain** about. I have no talent to show. Even if I did, I have no desire to throw myself before people for their applause.

—Rita Williams-Garcia, *One Crazy Summer*

violate (vī′ə lāt′)

verb

To fail to obey a law or rule: *The driver was fined for violating the speed limit.*

> Everyone in the school knew Linda Gold. If there was ever a list with kids who had done something or won something, you could always find Linda's name near the top of it. She was blond with gray-green eyes and a sprinkling of freckles around her nose. She also had a running battle with Miss Green, who accused her of **violating** the school rules by using lipstick.
>
> —Walter Dean Myers, *Darnell Rock Reporting*

vital (vīt′l)

adjective

1. Having to do with life: *The doctor checked the patient's temperature, pulse, and other vital signs.* **2.** Necessary for life to continue: *The heart and lungs are vital organs.* **3.** Very important; essential: *A good education is vital to a successful career.*

> I've pointed out time and time again how **vital** it is that one be able to read well. I've stressed on numerous occasions the importance of being familiar and comfortable with literature. Today Miss Henry and I would like to give you a demonstration of your own possibilities in this regard.
>
> —Christopher Paul Curtis, *The Watsons Go to Birmingham—1963*

vivid (vĭv′ĭd)

adjective

1. Bright and strong; brilliant: *Isaiah's new coat is a vivid shade of blue.* **2.** Active; lively: *You have a vivid imagination.* **3.** Sharp and clear: *We still have vivid memories of our trip to Washington, DC.*

> He looked back. For a minute he thought he heard a faint muffled bark, and it seemed as though the iron tail had started to wag. Mark guessed he must have a pretty **vivid** imagination, all right, the way Miss Amrhein, his last year's teacher, had always said.
>
> —Edward Eager, *Half Magic*

wistful (wĭst′fəl)

adjective

Full of or expressing sad yearning: *I wrote a wistful poem about homesickness.*

---

vivid / wistful

"Do we have anything to eat?" Pinch's voice was small and **wistful**; he sounded like a little boy, not the warrior he pretended to be. He sat down on a log, looking out over the lake, and scratched his head.

—Louise Erdrich, *The Porcupine Year*

yield (yēld)

verb

1. To give or produce something: *The fertile soil yielded a large crop. The improved process will yield better results.* **2.** To give something up; surrender: *The soldiers yielded the fort to the attacking army.* **3.** To give in; submit: *We yielded to their arguments.* **4.** To give way to physical pressure or force: *The soft dough yields when pressed with a finger.*

noun

An amount that is produced: *We hope to increase our yield of tomatoes this year.*

> "Very well, then," said the Badger firmly, rising to his feet. "Since you won't **yield** to persuasion, we'll try what force can do. I feared it would come to this all along."
> —Kenneth Grahame, *The Wind in the Willows*

zest (zĕst)

noun

1. Flavor or interest: *Spices give zest to simple foods.* **2.** Great enjoyment; relish: *Kevin ate his meal with zest.*

The Queen's class, left behind in school while the others scattered to green lanes and leafy wood cuts and meadow byways, looked wistfully out of the windows and discovered that Latin verbs and French exercises had somehow lost the tang and **zest** they had possessed in the crisp winter months.

—L. M. Montgomery, *Anne of Green Gables*

The 100 Words

accommodate
afterthought
allegiance
aloft
ancestor
anticipation
antics
apparel
ascend
beckon
brink
catastrophe
coax
compassion
complexion
content
courteous
cringe
derelict
dignity
distaste
dormant
elaborate
endure
enforce
exertion
expanse
extraordinary
foliage
foremost
frank
function
futile
gaze

glimmer
glimpse
grimace
headstrong
hesitate
hoist
immense
imperceptibly
indication
inscription
instinctive
intent
interior
jar
keepsake
knack
literacy
lurch
makeshift
malicious
massive
meager
melancholy
merge
mingle
minuscule
momentary
nape
nimble
obstinate
opt
overwhelming
pact
pandemonium

persuade
phenomenal
ponder
quantity
quaver
quench
radiant
ravine
recipient
resentful
satisfactory
sensitive
sentiment
shudder
sickly
sleek
solemn
soothe
stagger
stern
tantalize
temptation
transform
unscrupulous
vain
vengeance
violate
vital
vivid
wistful
yield
zest

Other Books in THE 100 WORDS ® Series

100 Words Every High School Graduate Should Know

100 Words Almost Everyone Confuses and Misuses

100 Words Every High School Freshman Should Know

100 Words Every Word Lover Should Know

100 Science Words Every College Graduate Should Know

100 Words to Make You Sound Smart

100 Words to Make You Sound Great

100 Words Almost Everyone Mispronounces

100 Words for Foodies

100 Words for Lovers

100 Words Every Middle Schooler Should Know

100 Words Almost Everyone Mixes Up or Mangles

100 More Words Every High School Graduate Should Know

From the editors of *The American Heritage® Dictionary of the English Language*, 5th Edition